SPY 101™

SECRET AGENT GEAR

SPY TOOLS & TECH: PAST, PRESENT, AND FUTURE

by Matt Payne

SCHOLASTIC INC.

>>contents

THE MOST MIND-BLOWING SPY TECH . . .

Security forces at the 2014 World Cup in Brazil will wear sunglasses with tiny cameras that can scan the crowd for the faces of wanted criminals.

>> a history of spy tech

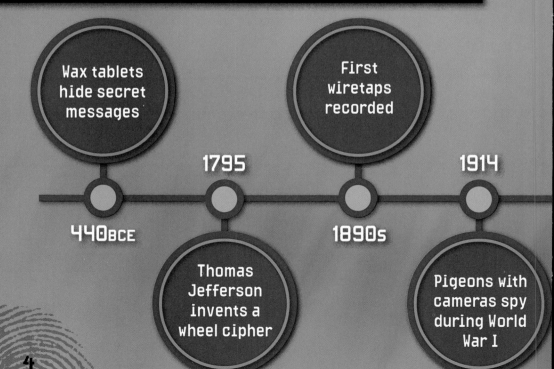

Wax tablets hide secret messages

440BCE

Thomas Jefferson invents a wheel cipher

1795

First wiretaps recorded

1890s

1914

Pigeons with cameras spy during World War I

OF ALL TIME!

Micro cameras! Face recognition! Science fiction is now spy fact. These glasses are just one of many unbelievable tech tools that spies use today.

Turn the pages to see many more cutting-edge spy gadgets and the latest spy tech—and see which tools have been used by spies throughout history.

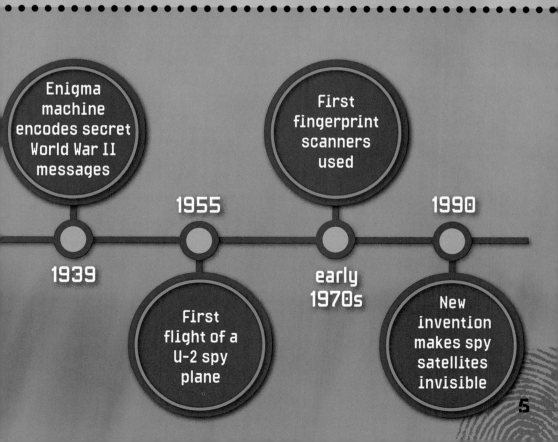

Enigma machine encodes secret World War II messages

First fingerprint scanners used

1955

1990

1939

early 1970s

First flight of a U-2 spy plane

New invention makes spy satellites invisible

section 1
SURVEILLANCE

SURVEILLANCE [sər-ˈvā-lən(t)s]:
Keeping a close watch on a suspect.

HELLO! IS ANYBODY THERE?

>>WIRETAPPING TECH Spies have been wiretapping since the telephone was invented—and were wiretapping telegraphs before that! Eavesdropping isn't new, but how spies listen in—and what they can hear—definitely is.

SPY LINGO

WIRETAP:
To listen to a private telephone conversation.

Voiceprint Recognition

WHAT'S A VOICEPRINT? >> Every person's voiceprint is unique—just like a fingerprint. So now spies can determine who's talking—even if the speaker doesn't say his or her name!

HOW IS A VOICEPRINT ANALYZED? >> The CIA and FBI can tap into the telephone switches that move millions of calls from one telephone to another, and use voiceprint recognition to detect criminal conversations. Voiceprints are analyzed using a combination of old-fashioned listening and machinery such as a sound spectrograph, which measures the frequency and intensity of the recorded speech.

● SPEECH **RECOGNITION**

OUTPUT LEVEL

0   30   60   90   120   150   180   210   240   270   300   330   360

6

People think that modern telecommunication is all wireless—but it's not. Even digital signals are supported by hardware housed in an office like this one.

Cell Phone Tapping

REMOTE TAKEOVER TECHNIQUES ≫

Spies have the power to turn any cell phone into a spy phone—even *your* phone!

Without ringing, cell phones can be silently turned on to listen in on any conversations happening around the phone!

HOW IT WORKS ≫ The latest smartphones contain everything from global positioning systems (GPS) to apps that track your footsteps, heart rate, and more. Tapping into these features is as easy as 1-2-3 for a seasoned hacker.

HISTORY OF SPY TECH

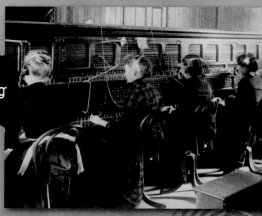

Wiretaps were first recorded in the 1890s, when the first working phone recorder was invented!

To make a phone call in the 1800s, you had to connect through a telephone operator. If they wanted to listen in, these operators could hear *everything*.

>> AUDIO SURVEILLANCE The word "bug" in spy-speak has always meant a small, hidden microphone that records secret conversations.

This fly (a bug), actually doubled as a spy bug (a transmitter/listening device); origin and date unknown.

Now, a bug could actually be a bug!

Here, Kitty, Kitty!

Perhaps the craziest bug ever created was a 1960s CIA project code-named "Acoustic Kitty." Cats were equipped with audio gear and sent to spy on Russian targets.

FAIL!

The project was quickly cancelled. Some of the cats simply wandered off. One spy cat was even hit by a car.

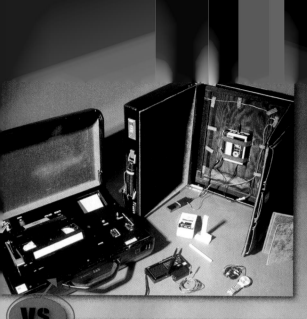

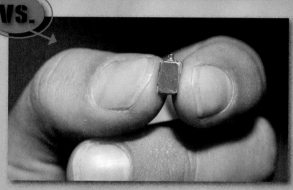

VS.

The Incredible Shrinking Recorder

Once spies have planted their bugs—they have to record what they hear.

Luckily for today's spies, recording devices are tiny.

During the Cold War, spies had to hide huge recording devices in their briefcases. Today, you can record conversations with a device that's smaller than your thumb.

Worried that you might be bugged?

Then grab a bug detector. Of course, if you have a bugged bug problem, then the best thing to do is set out a few roach motels!

HISTORY OF SPY TECH

Russian schoolchildren gave the American ambassador a handmade Great Seal of the United States. Inside—a bug! It hung in his home for years.

HERE'S LOOKING AT YOU!

>> THE TINIEST CAMERAS Today's spy cameras are unbelievably easy to hide. Fifty years ago, a spy had to carry around a very obvious, very large camera—and had to grip a massive switch to click a pic. Now the entire camera can be hidden in a button. How fashionable!

VS.

Camera in Glasses

It looks where you look!

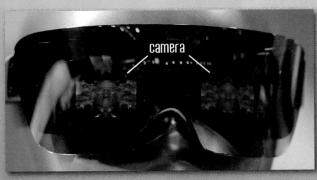

camera

SCREW hidden camera

Camera in the Head of a Screw

Beware the telephone worker visiting to install wires....

Pen Camera

As an added bonus, you can take notes!

Peephole Reverser

Although not a camera, a peephole reverser gives spies the ability to see into a peephole—from the outside of the door!

THE MIGHTY PIGEON TECH

Believe it or not, pigeons have influenced spy tech: In 1870, microdot photo technology was created because carrier pigeons couldn't carry large messages during the Franco-Prussian War. Messages were shrunk down into tiny photographs.

AN IMPORTANT SET OF SPIES HELPED THE ALLIES WIN WORLD WAR I— PIGEONS!

>> AIR AND SPACE SURVEILLANCE
Spy sky tech is getting smaller and more secretive, and the pictures look fantastic. So the next time you look up—say cheese!

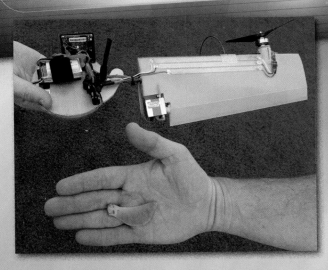

Top Sky Tech: MAPLE SEED DRONES >>

The latest drone tech can be launched with a flick of the wrist, and floats through the air like a big maple seed.

High-Flyin' Spyin': PLANES >>

Spy planes have been busy flying and spying since the 1950s. Here are stats on two of the most important:

LOCKHEED U-2 (AKA DRAGON LADY)
IN SERVICE: 1955 - CURRENTLY
LENGTH: 63 feet
WINGSPAN: 103 feet
MAX SPEED: 500 miles per hour
MAX ALTITUDE: 70,000 feet

LOCKHEED SR-71 "BLACKBIRD"

IN SERVICE: 1964–1998

LENGTH: 107 feet

WINGSPAN: 56 feet

MAX SPEED: Mach 3.3 (2,200 + miles per hour)

MAX ALTITUDE: 85,000 feet

Top Space Tech:
SATELLITES 》

Spy satellites take pictures and video, can see through clouds, and listen to enemy signals.

The Satellite Signature Suppression Shield makes satellites undetectable to enemies. When used, the satellite can't be seen from Earth!

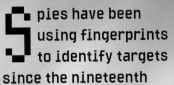

>>BIOMETRICS Unique physical traits used for identification, such as fingerprints.

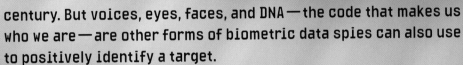

Spies have been using fingerprints to identify targets since the nineteenth century. But voices, eyes, faces, and DNA—the code that makes us who we are—are other forms of biometric data spies can also use to positively identify a target.

One booming biometric tech is facial recognition. This technology is available to just about anyone. Basic software on personal computers can be used to sort your personal family photos. More advanced algorithms are used by secret agencies and governments for covert activities.

The future of biometrics? Capturing biometric data fast and from far away. Technology is being created to scan faces from a distance, and while the target is in motion.

An iris scanner that can ID people in just one glance—at the rate of 30 IDs per minute—already exists!

Fingerprints can now be scanned from 20 feet away. (Better wear gloves!)

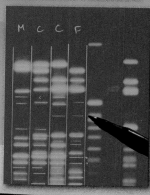

Meanwhile, back at the lab...
DNA FINGERPRINTING >>
Spies can now swipe a hair or saliva from the rim of a glass and send it back to the lab to positively identify a target!

BIOMETRICS: A FOOL-PROOF ALIAS-BUSTER

It's now harder for spies to have secret identities because of biometric checks at airports and seaports around the world. Facial recognition photography and fingerprinting are common at U.S. Customs checkpoints.

COVERT COMMUNICATIONS ['kō-(.)vərt kə-,myü-nə-'kā-shənz]: Passing along secret information without giving yourself away. Known to spies as "COVCOM."

KEEP IT SECRET. KEEP IT SAFE!

>> **HIDDEN INFORMATION** You're deep within enemy territory. How do you send your secrets home? Here's a look at the gear behind COVCOM.

SPY LINGO

DEAD DROP: Secret locations where a spy can leave secret information for another spy to pick up.

A newspaper left on a park bench might actually be a dead drop!

Dead Drops

These tools or locations allow spies to pass along information to one another without having to meet, which is often risky.

Dead drops can be anything—hollow bricks, a hollow spike you can drive deep into the ground, or even a trash can or the space under a bench.

Spies have even used the hollowed-out bodies of dead rats! Agents would sprinkle the rodents with hot sauce so cats wouldn't eat the dead drop!

Top Dead Drop Tech:
Fake Rock with Receiver

One agent wirelessly transmits information into the rock. Another agent picks up the rock and downloads the information.

Information on the Move

Along with the hollow coin and hollow pen pictured below, spies have used everything from hollowed-out teeth to shaving cream to smuggle information out of enemy territory.

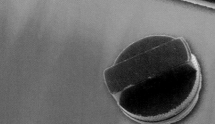

>> HIDDEN MESSAGES Your enemy can't find a secret message if they don't know it's there. Spies can hide secret messages in items that don't look like a message—a letter to Mom, or a picture of a tourist attraction.

Photographic Steganography

This photo shows a piece of ordinary film, just one millimeter in size, engraved with a holospot. A holospot is a modern version of the microdot and can hold up to one gigabyte of information.

Hidden images or text don't have to be digital. The simplest form of steganography is to simply hide information in an unlikely place, such as underneath a stamp on the front of an envelope.

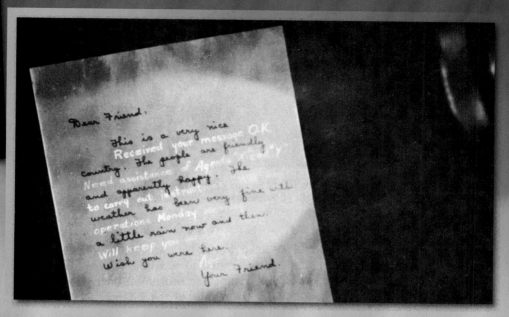

Another fun example of steganography: letters written with invisible ink. The messages are revealed under a black light, or when the paper is heated.

HISTORY OF SPY TECH

Steganography is one of the oldest spy tools. Its first known use was in 440 BCE—warning the Greeks of an attack!

WORLD'S STRANGEST STEGANOGRAPHY

1. Shave the messenger's head.
2. Tattoo a message on his head.
3. Wait for the hair to grow back.

>> SPEAKING IN CODES Writing in code is known as cryptology. A person who invents secret codes is known as a cryptologist and they practice encryption. A person who breaks secret codes is a cryptanalyst and they practice decryption. A key is used to determine how the message is encrypted and decrypted.

E-Mail Encryption Tech

Codes are extremely important in the age of the Internet—e-mail messages can be intercepted easily.

E-mails are encrypted into a series of numbers, letters, and characters based on a key. The encrypted message can only be read by someone who has the right key.

Cryptology Gear Through History

Founding Father Thomas Jefferson invented a wheel cipher in 1795. It has so many wheels that a modern computer has a hard time cracking the code!

The Enigma machine was used to encode secret German messages during WWII. It had 158,962,555,217,826,360,000 (that's 158 quintillion) different keys!

THE MIGHTY PIGEON!

In November 2012, a British family found a dead WWII carrier pigeon in their chimney. Attached to its leg was an encoded message that has yet to be decrypted!

section 3
CYBER ESPIONAGE

CYBER ESPIONAGE [ˈsī-bərˈes-pē-ə-ˌnäzh]: Spying on computer systems to gather secrets.

>> THE NEW SPYING THREAT

Every spy agency around the globe agrees on the biggest security threat: cyber espionage. Any computer connected to the Internet could have its information accessed by spies from anywhere in the world.

Cyber Gadgets

COUNTERFEIT COMPUTER PARTS >> Two computer parts might look almost exactly the same. But counterfeit parts can be built with software that will send any information on a computer back to cyber spies!

USB KEY SPYWARE ⟩⟩ A spy can force your computer to send all of its data to their computer by quickly inserting a USB stick loaded with spy software (known as "spyware").

RECORDING KEYSTROKES ⟩⟩
A Keylogger is used to record everything a user types into their computer—including passwords.

There are other ways spies can nab your password—decrypt encrypted wireless keyboard signals, detect keystrokes through electrical wiring, even monitor keystrokes with lasers!

THIS MESSAGE WILL SELF-DESTRUCT . . .

Worried spies might access your files? Just put them all on a self-destructing USB stick and if they try to grab it, one simple text message will fry the circuits!

ACCESS GRANTED

>> THE ART OF HACKING A spy who can access secret files on a computer using the Internet is known as a hacker.

So How Does A Hacker Hack?

First the hacker has to trick the computer user into downloading spyware.

One of the most common ways this is done is spear phishing. Spear phishing is when a hacker sends an e-mail that seems real to the user. If the user opens a file attached to the e-mail, or clicks a link in the e-mail, a RAT downloads onto the computer.

RAT is short for REMOTE ACCESS TROJAN, which is a type of spyware that allows the hacker to control your computer.

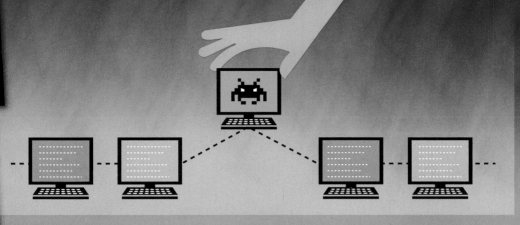

Not only can the hacker look at everything on your computer but your computer could be turned into a BOT.

A BOT is a computer that sends out countless spear phishing e-mails to even more computers, continuing the cycle.

What's the Password?

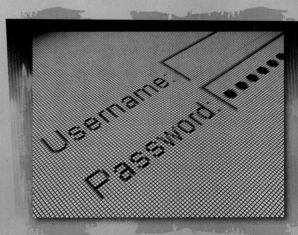

PASSWORD CRACKERS >>

A brute-force password cracker tries every letter, number, and character combination to guess your password.

UNCRACKABLE PASSWORDS >>

Use a longer phrase (ILovetoSpy) rather than a word-number combination (Spy123), and you'll have a much stronger password.

A 12-character phrase would take a brute-force password cracker 317 years to crack!

section 4
SPY GADGETS
FACT OR FICTION ACTIVITY

Hollywood Spy Gadgets

James Bond's Aston Martin spy car featured smoke screens, oil slicks, machine guns, and a passenger-ejector seat. Oh, and it looked really awesome, too!

Unfortunately for real-life spies, James Bond's spy car is not real—although both the CIA and Britain's MI5 (home to James Bond) have said they keep an eye on fictional spy tech for new ideas.

Some Hollywood spy gadgets sound like they could be real and some are outrageous:

Spy Kids' Hammer Hands

Inspector Gadget's Copter H

Then there's real spy tech that sounds like it should be from Hollywood: a lipstick pistol used by the KGB actually does exist!

So, now that you've studied up on spy tech, can YOU tell SPY GADGET FACT FROM FICTION?

Which of these four gadgets is for real, and which are Hollywood fiction (as far as we know)?

Write FACT or FICTION in the space next to each item, and then look at the next pages to see if you got it right.

Laser Wristwatch: _____

Remote-Controlled Shark:_____

Dragonfly Mini-Camera:_____

Telephone Shoe:_____

Laser Wristwatch: **FICTION**

A laser wristwatch has been featured in four Bond films. But laser beams aren't the only things Bond uses his watch for. He's also worn watches with grappling hooks, circular saws, homing devices, detonators, and more. Oh, and of course he sometimes uses the watch to tell time.

But there are real spy watches—they just don't have lasers. In 1949, the Germans devised the first camera wristwatch that took an astounding eight pictures at the time. It looked more like a wrist-camera than a wristwatch.

Remote-Controlled Shark: FACT

Several news agencies have reported that the Pentagon is researching shark brains. Their goal: learning how to control the sharks and turn them into "stealth spies." So, while not quite fact yet, it's in the works. The above image is an animatronic shark used in the *Jaws* films.

While the Pentagon waits for their spy sharks, they can always borrow the CIA's robotic catfish. Charlie doesn't have as many teeth, but he's very stealthy.

Dragonfly Mini-Camera: FACT

Dragonfly spies have been around since the 1970s, when the first INSECTOTHOPTER was created by the CIA (pictured above). It was gas-powered, and flew perfectly—unless it flew into any wind.

In 2008, a Dutch company by the name of DelFly created the smallest known dragonfly camera. It weighs only one-tenth of an ounce and has a wingspan of four inches!

Companies today are perfecting the art of the robotic bug. The "Micro Flying Robot" pictured below was invented by Japanese electronics company Seiko Epson Corp. The flight path of this small device can be controlled by a computer using Bluetooth. This special bug is perfect for use in security, surveillance, and disaster relief. So, the next time you hear a buzzing in your ear, smile for the cameras!

Telephone Shoe: **FICTION**

Get Smart's Agent Maxwell Smart is known for his wacky gadgets, and none is wackier than his telephone shoe. Some stores sell a telephone shoe as a joke, but no secret agent has ever used one. Why bother when you can call headquarters on a secure cell phone?

However, here's an interesting historical spy shoe — during the Cold War, several spy agencies created bugged shoes that would send radio transmissions back to spies.

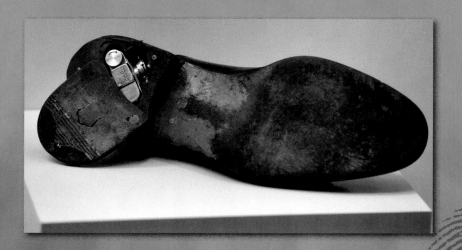

The Future of Spy Tech

History has shown that spies will always use the newest tech—even creating their own!

So, what's next?

Soon everything you own could be connected to the Internet. Load a movie on your big screen . . . while at school. Turn up the heat when it gets cold . . . from your bed.

But the more things are connected to the Internet, the easier it is for spies to get your information—and even control your stuff!

For instance, scientists have already hacked into the computer of an automobile in motion.

Now THAT would be an interesting car chase!